Unchain'd Inspiration

By
Damon Davis, Nomad the Unspoken Poet

PUBLISHED by PARABLES
Earthly Stories with a Heavenly Meaning

Unchain'D Inspiration
Damon Davis, Nomad the Unspoken Poet

Published By Parables
August, 2019

All Rights Reserved. No part of this book may be reproduced or utilized in any form or by any means, electronic or mechanical, including photocopying, recording, or by any information storage and retrieval system, without permission in writing from the author.

    ISBN 978-1-951497-31-6
    Printed in the United States of America

Readers should be aware that Internet Web sites offered as citations and/or sources for further information may have been changed or disappeared between the time this was written and the time it is read.

Unchain'd Inspiration

By
Damon Davis, Nomad the Unspoken Poet

PUBLISHED by PARABLES
Earthly Stories with a Heavenly Meaning

POETRY FOR PEOPLE IN LOVE WITH SUFFERING PRETENDING TO BE HAPPY.

By Damon 'NOMAD' Davis
The Unspoken Poet.

Dear Ms. Inspiration,
I hadn't realized that I'd lost sight of you in my minds eye
Til' the moment was upon me that I almost caved in under the
weight of anger & despair.
Rage was in the air.
Yet, the concierge of ignorance was unaware
That a change was coming,
The war cries within my soul were drumming
My heart pounding.
A hundred miles and running,
N.W.A
If I explode,
I'm D.O.A.
The loss of HOPE eventually will have sealed my fate.
PAUSE. Take a breath.
Maybe it's not too late for this naive C.O. to
Get OUT of HIS own WAY...Because it's hell to pay
If I lose it today.
I can hear you saying, 'I knew you didn't have what it takes If that's the case, Why bother in the first place.'
PAUSE. Take a breath. Thank God, I made it through another day.
UNCHAIN"D INSPIRATION, Let THAT
Be the reason I make it out of this place.

Special Thanks:
FOR ALL OF YOUR ENCOURAGEMENT
FAITH AND SUPPORT
ROSA FRAYRE
MINDEE MITCHELL-BROWN
DEREK VAUGHN
MICHELLE MEINBERG
SCOTT WILLARD
MS. C. WOODS
KATIE ANDERSON
M. WOODEN
AND OFFICER ROBERTSON

An endearing warriors salute to my brother and highly accomplished author Mr. William S. Graham for family is" who we choose". To celebrate my success is to celebrate his success. For it was his passion, focus and resilience that made this expression of my soul a "still-shot in motion" for the public to see. #Trendsetta's

Last but not least, a warm thank you to my dear friend, Donna Tortessi No. 172224 who herself is the perfect definition of "FRIENDSHIP AND BEAUTY"# Green Lives Matter.

ACKNOWLEDGEMENTS

THE SYNERGY OF HUMANITY
There is something harmoniously special to be said about the world's most unlikely and unheard of places of human suffering. One place in particular, which is rarely(if ever spoken of) except when reflecting on war times in ancient to modern history is a prison infirmary. I can tell you from first hand experience that working 40 hours a week, twenty-two days a month, in one of only two infirmaries in The State of Colorado for the past five years till this present moment, is that there is an oddly undiscovered culture of philanthropy, human kindness, and compassion one would never expect in a prison; let alone a level 5 facility such as The Denver Reception and Diagnostic Center. The presumed societal throw-a ways working side by side in synergy with societies number 1 healers to save life, preserve life, and often times the farewell companions to strange faces as they enter into the next stage of existence.

So here's to you! The nurses! The 12 hour days! Away from all you hold dear to be here! Especially the graveyard shift! If the rest of the world can't see you it's because they're sleep when you're on your feet! Your efforts will never go unrecognized by me!

Where there is suffering, there is pain. Where there is pain, there is need for healing. Where there is healing, there is (LOVE) of the highest magnitude found in humanness.

Loss and grief
A thief unbeaten
A virus sent to weaken the heart of the strengthened
A pot so sweetened
It's likened to misery and vulnerability
Just ask the people closest to me
Better yet,
Those who are estranged from me
No worries,
I'll pay my bounty
The reaper gets all that's owed to him eventually
Pain ever-lasting while you're living
And hell fire possibly when you leave
It's all apart of the plan if you ask me
But don't ask me
Because I don't believe in half of what I see
And it's even a far cry if I've ever heard anything correctly
So I fall to my knees and ask God to forgive me
Bless all those who've been hurt or deceived by me
The rest is a blur so I just keep on living
As I attempt to convert my arrogance into giving
Without losing confidence in who I am and the life I'm given
The Warrior must cut ties with anything that weakens his fighting spirit
But what's the use in all this fighting if at every turn they want me to lay down my weaponry
Me, in each environment, I operate differently
Strangely enough they don't want me to relinquish what I believe
They could care less about my rusty armor
Yes, it's best that I remain a fisher of men, divide the bounty
Then specialize in absconding
Not likely karma
Dharma
Malfunctioning
Grieving the loss most definitely
If I were to let external extremities internally affecting me
Respect me

Loss and grief
The nature of the beast
Lay it at his feet
Keep stepping
Put your faith in the power of a higher entity
HOLY DIVINITY.

Damon Davis, Nomad the Unspoken Poet

Dedicated to the Secret Society of LOVE

Lost Love
Instant Love
Strange Love
Taboo Love
Insane Love
Gangster Love
Sacred Love
Unconditional Love
Deep Love
Great Love
True Love
Free Love
Spiritual Love
Rekindled Love
Your Love
....for Love is Love

WARNING YOU MAY NEED TO CONSULT YOUR NEAREST PSYCHOTHERAPIST AFTER READING THIS.

INTRODUCTION
POETRY FOR PEOPLE IN LOVE WITH SUFFERING PRETENDING TO BE HAPPY.

The experts will say that," It's all in your head."
Strange, reflecting on such statements I can recall a conversation I had with a woman. She had been with her husband for several years. They had two young children.

We were discussing relationships, love, romance, infatuations etc. She said that much of her time was wrapped up being a mother and with work. She stated that her life was pretty routine; work, home, kids, cook, drink some wine, read a book, maybe get some nookie. Sleep and back to work all over again.
I said, "Damn. When is there ever time for the attention to be all on you."
Her reply, "Things change."

Impulsively, I said, not with me.
In my head I was thinking, maybe she married the wrong man or that she married for stability, something other than love as many couples do these days. So I asked her what she thought about love period and why she would candidly accept "Things change'. When it came to adoration & affection for her as a wife.

She said that she believed that LOVE was conditional. And that it was impractical, somewhat impossible even, to find a mate that was (all) things wrapped in one person. Someone who met (all) of ones physical, mental, and emotional needs. Your friend, your passionate lover, your companion, your husband, a great father etc.

I had to disagree. If it is rare, it's because individuals make it rare. The people. We've accepted mediocrity, lack luster and Luke warmness as the standard for our relationships.

Of course, everyone has their own idiosyncrasies that make them. However, I believe that you most definitely can find that intrinsic compatibility. A connection that never tires. That attraction that refreshes itself every time you look into your special someone's eyes. A feeling that is (unconditional) despite (any) external changes whatsoever. Feelings that only grow deeper & stronger with each new experience, good or bad.
I guess, one cannot miss what they've never had.

Honestly, I just wanted to prove to her that—that type of connection did in fact exist. More than anything I wanted to show her because, secretly. . .I longed for her in that way. Deep down morally, I knew it was wrong.
Or was it...

Had she married the wrong man? Or had she married the right man for the wrong reasons? Or was everything just perfect, it was all in my head and I was the one who was out of season?

Yet, it wasn't like I intentionally searched out of this type of arrangement. What drew us together wasn't by any power I alone possessed. From our first encounter I felt like I knew her. The feeling was mutual. Even she was puzzled. Nevertheless, at the very moment we met, I accepted any and all of her secrets, idiosyncrasies and the mystery that made her- her. However unexplored at the time, she was as familiar to me, as a very dear childhood memory.

Naïve...maybe

Well, here is its poetry.
But before we get into all that...
This is what she left me.

A QUOTE FROM BUDDHA:

"In the end, only three things matter:
how much you loved,
how gently you lived
and how gracefully you let go of things not meant for you."

Warmest,

Unchain'd Inspiration

A DEEP BREATH

The windows to my soul suddenly open
A breath of fresh air rushes in
Life fills my lungs
The warmth in my veins excites
As I unearth from my temporary resting place
Still engulfed in a blanket of serenity
A basin of fresh water awaits my presence

A deep breath...
I have risen
Blessed be the day I say
As I put on my garments for today
Freshly pressed, exhale all stress
For there is still much work to be done
Many challenges and great adventures lie ahead

A deep breath...
A smile parts my lips
While I sip coffee and clear my head
Timeless meditation

A deep breath...
Awwwweee, here we are again,
Unit 4 A
What a perfect place to begin
Click.
My cell door opens
The day is what you make it
Exhale I'm ready!

SPIRITUAL WARFARE

Dear Brother,
I was hoping to recognize you outside of the synagogue, the mosque, the temple. Yet, it is only in worship that I know you. Only in prayer are we a pair. Brother to Brother, one like the other none other than one who performs under a scope for appearances self righteous interferances claim our ego's in vain succession
But we'll be okay. The day is full of every opportunity to express greater unity, deeper levels of integrity if there is such a thing. In reverence. In fellowship. In worship.
I was hoping to embrace a deeper sense of what it meant to live in harmony with those next to me as we search within ourselves, The light of Divinity that will illuminate the path to destiny.
What a tragedy to talk this way and walk separately
BOOM!
RELIGIOUS CATASTROPHE.

All is fair in love and war

Unchain 'd Inspiration

She is the scope of my mind's eye
Though shameful am I
That she also be the symbol of hope & freedom that I long for
In the light of day, In dark of the moon
When my thoughts arise and my feelings swoon
Down on me to gloom
That a day doesn't come soon
For our hearts to bloom
In our own private moment
That her love comes down on me when she's on it
Soft and sweet as a Shakespeare sonnet
Lord forgive me
For the emotional places she's taken me
Like a pill of ecstasy
I'm intoxicated by our chemistry
When she's m—i--l-e-s a—w--a--y
I feel her next 2me
When she's by my side
I feel that she's apart of me
Unable to dispel the connection
I look at her and see my reflection
Polar opposites of what the people expect
Like OBAMA in the WHITE HOUSE after the presidential elect
So let the record reflect
That
THE WORLD IS SHADY
And there's more than just 50 shades of ME in my LADY
Yea
I'm sweet on her
I call her my sugar baby
WOULD I SETTLE FOR LESS
Maybe
If she was half the woman
With less than the man and they paid me
Naw

Unchain 'D Inspiration

Who am I kidding
I'd take HALF of her for free
Call it a blessing to be
Because the truth is
She's not actually with ME
Yet praise BE
To the magnificent magnetic force that compelled her soul to mine
It may be
The very source that sets me free
Surely we shall see
Indeed
Infinitely
My heart is CHAIN'D to thre
INSPIRED DEEPLY

By every vision
Every memory
That many may call a child like devotion
From an enchanted moment
Orchestrated
By some unlikely deity

Yet I laugh
And go at it blindly

Madly in love
I'm outta mind
Like sex without the glove

A willing sacrifice
For all that I dream of
Because

I'm a raving lunatic
For the one who makes my heart tick
If it stops
Then that's the tock
The last beat on my clock

At this point
There isn't anyone else in the world
That makes my heart knock
Poetically
I should stop

TRAPPED between two worlds'

It feels as if I was born to suffer

Then
I awake from the dream
Look in the mirror and say

"THAT'S ONE BAAAD MUTHA………."

Breathless in an OASIS 'Counting Crows'

When you left, my inspiration for artistic expression left with U
The color in my pencils began to fade. The true meaning of 50
SHADES OF GREY, when a person ceases to see the color in a
day.
I have a 50 pack of Crayola's and they all seem the same.
Someone reaches out to me, The warmth of the connection eludes
my senses. A STALEMATE.
Unable to feel the vibration beneath the breastplate.
CHECKMATE.
This is loneliness.
A bald eagle soaring, I'm living through it.
With a smile that glows, I'm a walking ray of sunshine.
For what woman can feel my heart,
What man can read my mind...
Last night, I searched for you on a GREEN DAY amongst
THE PAVEMENT, THE CRANBERRIES, THE BLACK-EYED
PEAS,
THE THIRD EYE BLIND and TOOL, wishing you were ONE
CALL AWAY
like CHINGY, that I could reach you. Instead, I settled in a
DREAM and awoke to find that my day was a little less stressful.
Inhale. Exhale. Just relax and let go.
Yes, I know.
Life will continue to blossom
And Love will continue to grow.
I can see you now...
Laughing, smiling,
Skiing the mountain slopes
Enjoying your children
Embracing your husband,
A life I may never know. Still.
I pray and I hope.
Contemplating...
I feel that God allowed me a glimpse of you in my life, that I
may know mercy. Allowed you to touch me with gentleness &
compassion, that I may know empathy.

That these examples be burned in my memory, That I may never astray from the path and purpose, That is meant for me.
An experience that lifted my lows' to a height that inevitably gave me WINGS, and maybe like MAYA ANGELO, This is why the CAGED BIRD SINGS...
FOR 'WOE' is "MAN" without everything that a WOMAN brings.

THE JEWELER'S CUT

Can a man ever truly find love while incarcerated
Temporarily incapacitated
In terms of fulfillment
With that special lady
Can a diamond ever be appreciated
While buried under miles of land
While we
On the surface
Are kicking cans
Cherishing contraband
With our feet surfing the sand
As a simple wave from a hand
Spells insignificant for the next man
JAIL BIRD.
For his dreams are still distant
Maybe even non-existent
Though his spirit spills of joy
What MADNESS!
Says the onlooker
Whose hands fasten tighter
Around her purse and windbreaker jacket
It's all just a rouse
His smiles
High spiritedness
Swagger
And humorous bullshit
THE CUT.
No wonder he's picky about with whom to share
His deeper thoughts with
Maybe
Over a bottle of ink or
Better yet
An OPUS ONE
A MARLOW
A 1936 BURGUNDY or

A ROMAN CONTI
And so many other things
She wouldn't expect from he
Simple in love
Strong in loyalty
Deeply embedded within the rose bush of intimacy
Oh NOW
She's addicted to ME
A DIAMOND IN THE ROUGH.
A distinctive CUT.
The rare JEWEL that lies beneath
Bars of earth
No matter what

The sparkle in my eye will always be

As the SUN casting its rays through
Shadows of men revealing
The mirror within her
That is me.

A BEAUTY that only the Beholder can see

THE JEWELER'S CUT

A SOULFUL CONVERSATION

There is no inspiration like love
No longing like loneliness
No loss like affection
No touch like tenderness,
(Here)
I've found deeper inspiration in motivational silence.
The eyes have a richer conversation
Than lips and persuasion
Where words travel like lost souls, forever lost
In translation.
Immediately, we intuit the truth.
Which is too RAW for most, and for others
Well...A little TOO uncouth.
The moment we have to explain,
We've engaged in a game.
Like children on a merry-go—round,
Designed to entertain.
SOULS UNTAMED
Soar like angels
While other's...
Lust for the slave master's reigns,
Puppeteer's on stage,
Simulating
Joy, love, and pain. Vague expressions.
Out staged
Outraged
By what lies beneath.
Choose me or lose me, Live Free or Die Hard, The prime opportunity.
Though it seems,
We were better off watching the movie
Than sitting face to face
Indulged in rhetoric
Beyond the scope of YOU & ME.
SHADOWS, PHANTOMS OF OURSELVES

We caress the mind
Pacify the heart
Avoid passion like the plague
Fill business with our day,
WE'VE BECOME THE WALKING DEAD.
INSTEAD.
We should sit in silence
And have a SOULFUL CONVERSATION

SINCERE DEVOTION

Today marks the moment in time
That my life and the days have been re-aligned
There is a song that my heart sings
Strings and melodies
It is an instrument of LOVE
An Orchestra
Of emotions
Feelings willed together
Manipulated at the finger—tips of one woman
No other woman
Can Don its keys
Nor play its tune
She strokes my heart with conviction
And plucks its strings with sincere devotion
I am DEVOTED to her touch and sensitive to her needs
Yielding indeed
We travel the world together

SINCERE DEVOTION.

Dear Love,
What are you searching for if LOVE is the ultimate goal,
unconditional and impartial. The glue that holds two people. Why
jeopardize that union
for one momentous melee of pleasure.
What else must the heart require,
What more must the soul desire,
If (all) cannot be found within the soul
(you) chose to help YOU GROW.
What additional vow must be taken,
What original vow was mistaken.
Clearly, Infidelity was not apart of the wholeness that you
Vowed to under DIVINE introspection, or...
Maybe it was and you married for ulterior motives.
Maybe you chose to compromise,
That small, yet unique part of YOU
That was innately the SOUL GLUE.
The SACRED FRUIT.
The passion that one claims will fade
Is the same passion, The Law of Attraction
That rises and takes hold of you
In the moment, that allows another to
Seduce You away from that which you vowed to.
You'll confess, It's just sex.
Then why not have it readily & often
With the ONE
YOU are ETERNALLY BOUND TO.
Sure, we can blame it on the movies, the need for excitement.
I'll say," Its The Law of Attraction, the pull of that passion fruit we
were advised in the beginning to hold on to."
You'll say," That culturally we have an excuse." Then I'll say, as
TD. Jakes,
O' WOMAN THOU ART LOOSED
And POOF!
I'm up in flames right next to you.

TELL ME...

TELL ME, What would it look like
If I was the only person that truly cared about your thoughts in eighteen years since you lost it all?
TELL ME, What would it feel like
If I was the only man who listened carefully, especially, after I was trained not to believe a word you ever said to me. Yet, I fought desperately for the information you entrusted to me?
TELL ME, What would it taste like
If I knew you wanted me like a Klondike, the feeling was mutual, but I told you maybe in the next life?
TELL ME, What would it sound like
If I held a glimpse of your freedom within my eyesight,
Would you get stage fright, act like it was all apart of the job... or indulge in a real moment of INSIGHT?
TELL ME,
Please.
I would really like to understand how it feels to live inside these PROFESSIONAL GUIDELINES...

PSYCHOTHERAPY.

IF ONLY
I
STOOD
ALONE

If only I stood alone,
I'd claim the victory
Call the Mountain my home
Bury my bone in three time zones as life goes on
I'd be ON like keynotes in the middle of a symphony.
If only I stood alone,
I'd take full responsibility.
Tell God, be cool.
Shake the Devil's hand
And call it Blasphemy.
Because I believe I can fly past all the suckaz' asking me,
What's my game plan,
Are you on your feet again,
What's the capacity.
If I only stood alone,
I could shake the partner's next to me
BE
Just like YOU.
A greedy hater
A selfish bastard
With nothing but the death of me.
Blind to success and The Law of Wealth
With nothing LEFT of Me,
IF ONLY
I
STOOD
ALONE.

ENOUGH.

AM I ENOUGH for you when we get through, Our passions fulfilled before and after the thrill. Will I still get chills when you cop a feel.
Just simple details I'd like to know to trust that its real.
Because I want to know what type of woman you really are.
I don't want to believe that you're a liar or a cheat. I want to believe that what we share is concrete.
You know how I feel about you. I know that you adore me, but am I one in a million or just one out of many
This cant be your first time feeling this way you do it much to easy. You have a delicate touch unlike anything sleazy. The way you finessed my thoughts and evoked my feelings. My heart was un-caged, you saw the real me. But, AM I ENOUGH for you.
In a time where women are all so greedy will you still need me after I've fulfilled my natural duty. Will you squander a KING'S RANSOM for any Tom, Dick & Harry. After multiple climaxes how much weight will each Dictation carry.

TRIVIAL PURSUIT.

POETRY SUCKS!

It's like Sap
Sticky to the touch
It's only sweet
When inspired to be such
BOILING POINT.
As maple becomes
Out of the emotional muck
Like syrup to pancakes
It's salve to the heart
Still

POETRY SUCKS!

Sucks the life right out of whoever it touches
Like ink from the pen
Drip by drip used
Over and over again
And still
One will never stop writing whatever needs to be written
Despite the fact that
It hurts the fingers and cramps the hands

POETRY!

We continue to demand
INSPIRE me!
FILL me!
TAKE me ON A JOURNEY!
ROMANTICIZE me!
Away from this nightmare I'm living
ENCHANT me with LOVE & SPIRITUAL FEELING
FREE me!
I'll pay!
I'm willing to do anything

Tell me lies
Smack me with truth
How swiftly POETRY salutes
As if sworn to obey you
No thought given to
All the moisture ciphered from the poets eyes
That were once so beautiful
Or
The smile that was all so charming
And once so colorful

POETRY SUCKS!

I'm up to my ears full!
Cut them off and still my soul pulls
I pluck my eyes out! Still
A vision awakens me
Please
Take my heart
Bleed the life out of me
I beg of thee!
Where must I flee?
Without its stench trailing me
Cologne
Perfume
Pap-e-lapue-achuuu!

POETRY
It reeks of warmth, tenderness and empathy

STRENGTH
WISDOM
And reverence of DIVINITY
For who speaks
Of the worlds beyond galaxies
Dimensions
Quantum leaps beyond humanity
Atoms and Eve's

Sunsets beyond the APPLE TREE
Unimaginable paintings

Brush strokes without fingertips
Artistry
Without rose hips
O' how life springs forth from pure BLACKNESS
And why all the colors of the rainbow seems to fit
How its light lit, by the very edge of DARKNESS

Naww man, POETRY SUCKS! I get this!

An indomitable bliss
For those who bare witness
To the details within the madness

For other's sadness
Unable to see beyond their noses
The world pities them

Yet for me
POETRY!

The world dares not look at me
MY LIFE'S PORTRAIT
Is not as pretty as they pictured me

Villainous. Ugly

Yea, it SUCKS to be me

POETRY.

"A Coward is incapable of exhibiting LOVE It is a prerogative of the BRAVE."

-Mahatma Gandhi

THERE IS NO ONE ELSE

I am who you seek to find when your heart is lost in the wilderness
of unhappiness. So come to me willingly. Hold my hand and I will
guide you back to a familiar place...
Where your heart is content, your lips love to smile, and your mind
is at peace
unwavering in the journey of life.
Where each moment spent holding my hand is a moment spent
in confidence and happiness
THE LIGHT.
In the midst of emotional darkness, confusion, and sadness.
You will never lose your way as long as you hold my hand.
I am the MAP to your treasure,
That precious HEART
That you tend to extend without measure
In the midst of scavengers & thieves
Who rip apart your flesh for their personal pleasure
They are WOLVES
That smell the scent of your emotions upon your sleeves
They swear in the name of LOVE & Guidance
Yet their path only deceives.
IT IS I IN TRUTH
Who
Will always answer your call
Respond to your touch
Respect your kiss and understand the thoughts
That mean so much.
So reach for me..
Hold my hand, let me lead the way
And you'll never go astray. I am your friend
your partner
your lover
Trust in our connection
Respect the Creator
And we'll need no other protection
IF you BELIEVE in what we

have, then you've just witnessed
A TOUCH OF GOD'S PERFECTION.
THERE IS NO ONE ELSE.

WITH YOU

With You, in this moment I am closest to GOD
when you are flowing through my veins.
With You, how is it possible that I cannot picture anyone
else in light of my embrace. I am unable to concentrate My
thoughts fixated on freedom in a way that reveals my selfishness
I only want to be free to be with you.
With You, I want to experience what it feels like being caressed by
your fingertips, slayed by your gaze...My body
christened by your lips as you offer yourself to me.
With You, I will respect your every wish, your every curve I will
rule with strength and grace. Your hearts' desire will
never be misplaced, as my hands will never betray to retrace
another.
WITHN YOU, In this moment.
I am closest to GOD.
FREEDOM means nothing without you.
This separation has my soul leaking,
Without you,
I will remain TRAPPED in a cage with all of my R bs M ss ng
Empty.

VACANCY

The rocking chair waddles back and forth flirting between kisses...
The wind is gentle, seductive.
The sky filled with envy
sends down warm—wet kisses of its own.
Tickling the back, sides, and seat of the rocking chair.
She giggles in amusement moving slower, sassier than before.
She's always eager to receive the company of a close friend or
distant relative. Especially, on days like this, Come. Sit. Picture
your favorite sunset,
With.
A warm kiss and a gentle breeze
So many great memories shared,
So much wisdom passed on from generation
To generation.
The rocking chair
Greeting each new guest
With a smile and an open heart.

VACANCY.

THE INNER CITY BLUES

It's Sunday. I'm lying on the top rack looking out the window as all the vehicles leave the parking lot, exiting the facility. I wonder who is in each car, van, or truck. I wonder what they are thinking, what they are saying. Which C.O.'s are going home to a family, a wife, and children. Or which ones are headed to some other destination.
I contemplate what it must feel like to leave this place after an eight hour shift into the embrace of the ones you love, that person anticipating your arrival. Be it a child screaming mommy, daddy! Or a husband or wife checking for one another. . .I envy them.
I wonder if it will ever be me coming home to someone's embrace. Will my children still need and want me. Will there be some other person who longs for my presence. Will my parents still be alive.
I am drifting now...The rain is coming down in what seems like slow motion. Ironically, the song 'Slow Love' softly plays in the distance. My mind is frozen in time.., my soul longs to be free from captivity. Yet somehow I feel good in my own skin, at peace not fully taken over by despair. Maybe it's a greater since of love than loneliness.
I am thinking of you...
I'm wondering if you made it home safely in the rain... If its wetness touched your face causing you to squint, making your make up run, and the curls of your hair become straight or tangled. I wonder what your first thoughts were when you stepped into the coziness of your home, in from the chill, safe from harm...was your body aching from the long work week? Who was there to massage your feet, your body, melting your tension away...
Well...It's getting late and my heart is truly beginning to get heavy. I have to end this journey outside my window and return to the reality of this top rack. I must get some rest, replenish my strength. For tomorrow the battle continues...and I must fight this fight till my freedom is in sight and I'm standing in it.

Right then, is when they will place me alongside the other GREAT MEN who changed the world, that were once in prison, INNER CITY BLUES DRIVEN.

IF (if) WAS A FIFTH

IF
it was my intention to impress you with words
I would simply offer you my heart and let it speak
for itself.
IF
I were to tell you exactly what's on my mind
I would fasten your lips to mine, intoxicate your space
escape this place, from the tip of my tongue to somewhere
deep within your waist, penetrate your mind, then ask you
how does it taste
hoping to clear your conscience where you kept me safe.
IF
I were to express my feelings
I would explode with emotions
expose your intense desire
and my deepest devotion, make reality our dreams
instead of caressing myself with thoughts of you
as a mechanism for coping.
IF...

FIRE DOWN UNDER VS. HOLY MATRIMONY

What good are my talents if I am uninspired
What good are gifts without anyone to receive
For all of my inspiration is within the arms of another man for how will she receive my gifts when he is giving her all that he can
Why is her appetite so insatiable and mine so unquenchable
FOR HER,
I would do the unthinkable
Only thinking of her OCTAPUS and my TENTACLES
Her suction cups are unbelievable!
When she sucks I bust
When she moans I thrust
OUT OF CONTROL,
Where I am is unconceivable. Whatever she wants I surrender two
Number two,
Its something hard to get use to when I'm the number one prick she loves to get loose to

HOLES IN MATRIMONY.

IN LOVE WITH SUFFERING PRETENDING TO BE HAPPY

There is a story in my heart tucked so deep that every time I think of it.. .Every time I pick up the pen to let the ink drip its life upon the paper...the pain brings me to tears, a lump forms in my throat, and my heart slows down like a heavily sedated patient about to undergo surgery.
At first thought, my impulse is denial.. .some mental game that I attempt to play with myself, as if to say its not real... It never happened, I don't care, we never met.. .or we did, yet the experience was absent and what I felt was false— imaginative bullshit.
Then.., in the silence, I realize that I am alone.. .and its okay to reveal my pain. Its okay to admit to myself that we did meet and it was real. That I felt every bit of your energy vibrating within me. A channeling of two beings in one body experiencing the same thing.
RIPPED from this timeline I'm left aching.. .A longing in every nerve and cell membrane.
See! People talk that shit about; what they WILL or WONT do when eclipsed in a connection like this. I've heard the comments. You're a fool, a simp, a square, shit like that doesn't exist.
Well, ain't that a bitch. Yeah, just bust a nut & get it over with. Procreation idiot.
Well, clearly you've misinterpreted me...
It's not about being deprived of mushy. I could have as much mushy that pleases me, but I don't want-just anyone's mushy. I want yours exclusively. I want to sample your juices, to taste what's in store for me beyond my pipe dreams of endless streams of your womanhood spilling over me.
I want to experience everything in The instincts in the way you look at me. That thing.
That makes you desire me uncontrollably. That silent something. That keeps you Coming back to me shamefully, like, 'How could this be happening when I am married happily.'
So alive in this fantasy that if you live for me, I'd die for you gladly.

After we've combined our chromosomes in a whirlpool of madness, I'd bathe in a shower of your golden essence, drink of your orgasmic pleasure on a scale that only U & I could measure You'd let me melt in your mouth like chocolate syrup on your favorite sundae. Just to repay the favor, you savor every inch of me Yeah. Because I'm THAT MAN! Mr. Mr. Nasty! one, to two steps above classy. Deeply in love with suffering pretending to be happy.

PIPE DREAMS...

"Love, you see, is the one force that cannot be explained... cannot be broken down into a chemical process. It is the beacon that guides us back home.. .when no one is there.. .and the light that illuminates our loss. It's absence robs us of all pleasure.. of our capacity for joy. It makes our nights darker.. .and our days gloomier. But...
When we find LOVE.. .no matter how wrong.. .how sad.. .or how terrible.. .we cling to it. It gives us our STRENGTH. It holds us UPRIGHT. It feeds on us and we feed on it."

-SETRAKIAN
First Season, THE STRAIN

GOD'S GREATEST GIFT TO MAN IS MUSIC & WOMEN

The anatomy of a woman is like a smooth groove
R&B on the move
A soul soothe with a little bit of blues should you pick & choose the right woman for you.
Believe me, I know what it do.
when a man is gone off the deep end she'll get him through
Rap, Jazz, new or old school.
Her body is a classical symphony
A tune we men seem to magically compose to

MUSIC TO MY SOUL
uplifting my spirit as she massages her rhythm into my temple
'Don't fight the feeling' sounds so simple
When I'm a raging bull her touch brings peace to my mental.
Without her I'd BURN like Usher in this hell hole
So I plug in and go H.A.M.
That way I don't feel so desperate and alone
Melodies of her anatomy keep me in a zone
Lyrics down to the BONE.
I'm on.
WORK, WORK, WORK. Like DRAKE & RHIANNA
Til 'the morning comes.

What say you ?

I internally verbalize the feelings I get when thoughts of you arise inside. Time speeds up then miraculously drags me by like a tide crashing upon the beach to patiently beseech all the interesting details back to the sea if need be.
A refreshing exchange from the summers' heat. A brief evade. The oceans retreat. However so subtle and discrete, this is the crest in which the souls meet.
Needless to say I miss you dearly. I am suffering without you yet it must be a mercy...
I'm praying for the Lord to reimburse me with someone equally endowed with your spiritual beauty. Am I selfish. Maybe. Or maybe I'm supposed to be, with all the things that were meant for me.
Aren't I supposed to cherish , appreciate, to count my blessings But.. how could I forget...
I am stripped from you by the sin of covet ness and you from me. For it takes Two to get in this mess, though it is I who is left with the shortest stick, You still have your husband. Your emotional affair remains a secret, with such a magnetic pull; I pray you'll be able to keep it.

Unchained Inspiration,
I wish you the strongest of love,
The best of happiness, and the deepest of passion
Because I want for you what I want for myself .Most of all,
I want what is meant for me only. ONLY
My heart CONVICTS me.
I am guilty,
With you is where I truly want to be...

DEAR LORD, save my soul from drowning.

WHAT SAY YOU?

H
I
G
H
RISK

Hi, you don't know me but...My name is LOVE. In case you were wondering, I was forged in darkness, shaped
in lonely hearts. Abandonment adorned me- kissed me passionately. I caved in to deceit, it's spell was so sweet. It's intimacy left clouds under our feet as a stride of elegance swept me into a soulful retreat where a hurricane stood waiting...
Here, I bowed humbly at the flood of blood pulsing thru my veins, caressing the overly sensitive nerve- endings of my sanity.
Endorphins exploding, filling 'open wounds' with the divine.
'This essence' beyond the physical presence, dissipated the instinct of self-preservation. And...
THOUGH WE SWAM THROUGH THE VALLEY OF LIFE
I SHALL FEAR NO VAGUE IMITATION.
Stranded in the waste lands of man & woman, here.
I am an alien.
LOVE.
The truth.
The sacrifice, that no one dares pay the price.
LOVE.
Abundant.
Genuine.
Deep and ultimately FREE...
Baby, I'm HEAVY.
Maybe that's why LUST, IMPATIENCE, and INSTANT
gratification seem to TRIUMPH over me. Where's the Victory...
Bountiful are the 'WELLS' of the superficial. Dry, and highly undrinkable are the 'WELLS' of well... Let's say, The HIGHLY huggable, greatly lovable with depths unbearable— heart throbbable, vision impairable, emotionally intoxicating—
pressure—busts-pipeable, passionately intense individual.
0' how I'm punished for speaking the unspeakable!

LOVE.
A harvest unreapable.
HERE. Isolation is my tormentor & peace bringer when my heart beats me to death. Senseless, unable to expel another breath. Still.. .L0VE RESUSCITATES.. .It has something left. Shhh, quiet! The earth is quaking, my ears are RINGING, I hear whispering!
Ahhh. . .Just another soul whispering my name in VAIN.

Hi, you don't know me but…

I ONLY WANT WHAT'S MINE

Dear Life
Dear Love,
I am searching for my higher thoughts...
I am wondering why God made me the way that I am.
This Face
This Body,
Moreover,
Why my mind thinks the way it does...
More honestly,
Why my heart LOVES the way it LOVES...
It holds on when life says, "Let go.."
It's loyal,
When those whose company it prefers...
Has long left.
So what's left.
Well
There are many blessings to count
But that's not what I'm counting about.
I'm counting the right, that
Every human being has the RIGHT
The FREEDOM, to love whom they will
To
Express
How they feel.
Which, Usually unfolds in circumstances that aren't Truly ideal.
At least,
That's what's real from my side of the field.
I FEEL...
That I am a magnet for bad habits,
ADULTERY.

PHANTOM CHASER

My soul longs for you.
Come rescue me, my black queen.
I need you Desperately
No longer can I fight the feeling,
Life's too Short, there's not much left of me.
I've tried money, cars, numerous broads,
Even Life Behind Bars.
Still I'm left with gaping wounds and Ghetto scars.
—Nothing fulfills my existence,
My life's partner is somehow missing,
Chasing empty visions.
I know the essence, but I've lost the image.
Speak to me!
I swear, I'll listen.
My mind is ready and my heart is willing.
I apologize for the times my anger was so unforgiving.
The pain-unrelenting, heartbreak—ending.
I had to stand on what I believed in.
I would feel unworthy if I stood on anything less than.
"Soul Sista",
I am more than a circumstance.
Tell me baby,
When was the last time your soul danced?
My sentiments exactly.
And until you come back to me,
I'll be a PHANTOM CHASER... Till I meet the other half of me.

To whom it may concern,

It's burning season
My heart torches whom ever it seizes
It pleases beyond expectational reason
Some would say it's too empathetic toward the feeling of
Treason.
Addicted to warmth,
Its hard to believe him
Over laden by truth
So most people leave him.
People addicted to freezing and temporary breezes of what they
feel is needed, though out of time & out of season.
Complacent behavior.
Let that be the reason,
Abandonment.
That the burden be too great to bear
For a brother,
A sister, or
The child with grandchildren.
-Family
Yet, in a room full of strangers
Who could compare, a sucka to a square...
Believe me,
No one would dare.
Except he who holds it altogether when no one is there.
Was it his clothes.. .his shoes.. .or the smile that he wears... That
seem to hide so well the emotional tares sewn to his soul shinning
like gold he was told. smile.
A statement to the world
That he refuses to fold.
To Whom it may concern, where am I

I'M AT HOME

IN A HOUSE OF CARDS

ALONE,

IN A PRISON VISITING ROOM.

WHEN THE SUN SETS I HAVE NO REGRETS

My days and nights are merged.
Just as the affinity of Life & Death.
I am a warrior who has fought countless battles.
I have grown weary yet my journey to salvation is not over.
Though it seems, never-ending.
I have heard men say, "That a coward dies a thousand deaths, A soldier dies but once."

I AM GREATER THAN THIS.
A PHOENIX
I have died a thousand times over yet I live evermore. The fact that I merely exist for some divine purpose beyond this flesh and blood, is a rationale that continues to elude my ordinary state of consciousness.
There are moments along this road that twist & tear at my insides so much that I want to give up this guest, Put an end to the suffering.
Yet, like the carrot dangling in front the horses mouth.. .I continue on despite the hunger pains.
THIS LIFE. THIS LOVE.
I MUST TASTE IT!
BUT...
I no longer trust love over my OWN instincts. Other's feelings over my PERSONAL experience.
My choices WILL not be motivated by circumstances.
MY WILL-WILL
Saturate my EVERY step.
For I am ALONE.
LOVE has left me to fend for myself, sword & shield,
Hand in hand, like the Gladiator. A SLAVE TO destiny.
YET,
Weep not for me.
For I TOO, HAVE LEFT.
Left your sympathy and your love to fend for themselves. They are the same, "WITHOUT ACTION"

I have no need nor desire for either of them.
Time means nothing, yet, my moments are precious.
I must move on,
FAREWELL...
For there will be another sunshine.

RAINDROPS AND WATERFALLS

When the anger & frustration subside
The tide of my emotions rise like tears of the sun
Spilling over the horizon
SHIPWRECKED.
A lost treasure in the Bermuda Triangle.
SUNKEN.
As the sparkling sands flicker a glitter of what's left of my bones,
Warm currents massage my soul with memories of how many loved me as long as I was on, and how many died with me the very moment I was gone.
Resurrected in the deadliest catch
A basket of crabs clattering
SILENCED,
Only by the sound of their shells shattering
Being devoured by another human being in luxury & plenty
RICH
With envy
Gossiping about how they really felt about me.
"Young black and beautiful or young black and ugly" With Titanic Extravagance they ENJOYED every inch of me
REGURGITATED PRAISE FOLLOWED BY DEFECATED loyalty
Please.
Spare me the pleasantries.
I'd rather lie HERE undetected by history, deep thoughts, and Misery,
Superficial to the life of me.
A BLACK DIAMOND
A RARE JEWEL
A LOST TREASURE
IMPRISONMENT
RAINDROPS AND WATERFALLS.

TIMELESS MEDITATION

Sitting in full-Lotus
Engulfed in the burning flames of Karma
Destiny awaits patiently...
Adversity is my teacher
Experience is my master, training my inner being to sit peacefully amongst the Flames
To emerge Fearless is my goal and the ultimate Beginning to truly living
SHINNING
Glimmering is the sight of birth
As my spirit is reformed.
GRACE POURS IN and my mind is stripped from bondage,
Desperately fleeing from its past and present impurities
ALAS'
My HEART is revealed!
Severed from the opprobrium of PRIDE, CALLOUSNESS and the UNFORGIVING TORMENTS of loneliness
Submerged in the intrinsic energy of LOVE.
Intense, unrelenting,
Mellifluous, quiescent
Unable to contain my impulse to speak I questioned it
Asking the flames to ease up a bit,

"The path to peace only hurts for a moment it responded."
EMBRACE YOUR FREEDOM
EMBRACE YOUR FREEDOM
The voice of Consciousness resounded.
When I opened my eyes
The penitentiary walls had dissolved
And there I was.., peacefully in the arms of my beloved.

FOREVER GRATEFUL

To the GLUE, my BROTHER
Charles Brim, Iris & Family.
You are the BROTHER in BROTHERHOOD, the SPACE
between the letters in FAMILY.
Thank you for keeping me relevant
In your heart and outside
These dark walls.

Ecclesiastes

Damon Davis, Nomad the Unspoken Poet

Unchain 'D Inspiration

Damon 'NOMAD' Davis